TRUMP CATS

This edition first published in Great Britain in 2016 by Orion
an imprint of the Orion Publishing Group Ltd
Carmelite House
50 Victoria Embankment
London EC4Y 0DZ
An Hachette UK Company

1 3 5 7 9 10 8 6 4 2

A CIP catalogue record for this book is available from the British Library.

Picture credits: Brian Roberts: page 86/7; Julyan Bayes: page 61; Andrew Hayes-Watkins:
page 51; iStock: all other images. Hairpiece photographs throughout: Alamy/Rex

ISBN: 978 1 4091 6782 2

Printed and bound by CPI Group (UK) Ltd, Croydon, CR0 4YY

www.orionbooks.co.uk

HUGH JANUS

TRUMP CATS

LACK OF
↓

THE WIT AND WISDOM OF
DONALD TRUMP
AS TOLD BY CATS

INTRODUCTION

America is angry. There is frustration with the system, fury at the so-called economic recovery, despair at foreign policy, fear of terrorist attacks and cataclysmic divides on immigration. Donald Trump vents this rage and has right-wing America purring with excitement, while liberal America, who saw nothing but a bad joke in his initial candidacy, now well and truly have their claws out for him.

But it always starts as a joke, doesn't it? America, land of opportunity, has a rich history of seemingly unlikely statesmen conquering a complete and utter lack of nous and suitability for office to soar over the political landscape. Trump just wants to be another cat who got the cream.

Political commentators have wondered what the world would look like with Trump in power: disastrous relations with the Middle East, an America full of gun-toting citizens, a refusal to address the environmental carnage we're inflicting on the planet, a deep suspicion of China and disenfranchised Muslim factions within society — all of which sounds really awful until you realise that it pretty much describes the world in which we already live.

Over the years Trump has offended women, gays, 'the blacks', Mexicans, Muslims, environmentalists, celebrities, the Chinese, the Pope, almost all of his political opponents and, some estimates claim, the entire population of Scotland. Yet people still love him. People still vote for him. And why? Because he's the top cat. He's not the kind to roll over and have his tummy tickled or waste time toying with a political ball of yarn; instead he says things like, 'We'll beat the shit out of ISIS.' Finally, we have a politician unafraid to use the word 'motherfuckers' when discussing international relations.

He's greedy, too – greedy for America. And, well, yes, for Donald Trump too. He makes Gordon Gecko look like a lunch-eating pussy. He'll be keeping the women and the property empire to himself, thank you very much, but he wants America to be on top again, to be the biggest, richest kid in the playground.

They say we get the leaders we deserve, and how can we argue when it comes to Trump? He is an internet troll with a hairpiece. And this is Donald Trump's personal pussy riot of offensive rhetoric. It's not so much a compendium of his Wildean wit and wisdom as it is a litter tray of the shit he shovels by a man who sees himself as the cat's pyjamas. This book isn't for the easily offended – you'll be sure to cough up hairballs in outrage – but for those of us who can still see the funny side, it is sure to provide a welcome dose of catnip . . . until the unthinkable happens and he becomes Mr President, the ultimate fat cat.

66

I've said if Ivanka weren't my daughter, perhaps I'd be dating her.

99

Which doting father can honestly say they haven't got a gag about banging their own daughter?

You know, it doesn't really matter what the media write as long as you've got a young and beautiful piece of ass.

Trumps and ass go together like a prenup and a combover.
From an interview with Esquire, 1991.

Robert Pattinson should not take back Kristen Stewart. She cheated on him like a dog & will do it again – just watch. He can do much better!

Dear Donald, a relationship and life advice service coming to a Twitter feed near you.

> I dealt with Gaddafi. I rented him a piece of land. He paid me more for one night than the land was worth for two years, and then I didn't let him use the land.
>
> That's what we should be doing. I don't want to use the word 'screwed', but I screwed him.

Trump lays out the practicalities for dealing with dictatorships as part of his foreign policy: screw 'em on real-estate deals.

It's Friday. How many bald eagles
did wind turbines kill today?
They are an environmental
& aesthetic disaster.

*Without a state-funded Trump combover programme for the bald eagle, it seems
likely that it will continue to be an aesthetic disaster when maimed in wind turbines.*

26,000 unreported sexual assaults in the military — only 238 convictions. What did these geniuses expect when they put men & women together?

Don puts forth his ideas for crime prevention in an apartheid society.

@ariannahuff is unattractive both inside and out. I fully understand why her former husband left her for a man — he made a good decision.

Don finally finds some common ground with the liberals as he embraces a same-sex relationship.

Our great African American President hasn't exactly had a positive impact on the thugs who are so happily and openly destroying Baltimore!

Yeah, why can't a black man tell other black men what to do? Don't these brothers listen?

I have a great relationship
with the blacks.

*He means Mr and Mrs Black, of course, his well-to-do white
neighbours and campaign contributors in Manhattan.*

Is filthy rich inner beauty or outer beauty?
Or is it just an all-round radiant glow?

I beat China all the
time. All the time.

*China is the pet name for his penis, the
real rising superpower always on The Donald's mind.*

It's freezing and snowing in New York — we need global warming!

Just like there is for the Bible, there are many interpretations of objective, empirical scientific data, and Donald's beliefs are just as valid as the next right-wing loon's.

I have never seen a thin
person drinking Diet Coke.

He should know – it's his favourite tipple.

You know what a gun-free zone is to a sicko? That's bait.

Bring-your-gun-to-school day certainly sounds like fun,
but he's sure to lose the sicko vote on this.

@Lord_Sugar – unlike you, I own *The Apprentice*. You were never successful enough...

The 'special relationship' between the UK and US takes a beating with **The Apprentice** bosses. Gentlemen, put your handbags away – you can't fire each other.

As everybody knows, but the haters & losers refuse to acknowledge, I do not wear a 'wig'. My hair may not be perfect, but it's mine.

Yes, Mr Trump, but have you considered investing in a wig? Or even just a hairbrush?

I don't have a racist
bone in my body.

*But we don't know the attitude of his organs. And didn't he have
a bone to pick with the Mexicans about something?*

No more massive injections.
Tiny children are not horses — one
vaccine at a time, over time.

*Once again, The Donald takes on science and prevailing medical wisdom
with the expertise built up during a career in real estate and television.*

Donald J. Trump is calling for a total and complete shutdown of Muslims entering the United States until our country's representatives can figure out what is going on.

Don's vision of collaboration is to refer to himself in the third person. It's a team effort, after all, and he's not going to be able to keep out all those Muslims single-handedly.

One of the key problems today is
that politics is such a disgrace.
Good people don't go
into government.

Finally, a moment of clarity.
It's never too late to get self-aware, Don!

On exporting goods to China:
'Listen you motherfuckers, we're
going to tax you 25 per cent!'

Diplomacy, Trump-style, motherfuckers.

The concept of global warming
was created by and for the
Chinese in order to make U.S.
manufacturing non-competitive.

*Forget the science — it's a Chinese conspiracy. Quick, throw out
pretty much everything you own and buy American!*

If you can't get rich dealing
with politicians, there's something
wrong with you.

Trump magic-markers the word 'sucker' across his brow for his life in politics.

If and when the Vatican is attacked by ISIS, which as everyone knows is ISIS's ultimate trophy, I can promise you that the Pope would have only wished and prayed that Donald Trump would have been President.

Trump's response to the Pope's questioning of his faith, prompting a new line of rhetorical questioning after 'Is the Pope a Catholic?' Is Trump a Christian? Does a Trump shit in the woods? If a Trump shits in the woods and no one is around, does it make a smell?

The Mexican government and its leadership has made many disparaging remarks about me to the Pope, because they want to continue to rip off the United States, both on trade and at the border, and they understand I am totally wise to them.

It was those pesky trash-talking back-stabbing Mexicans to blame after all – of course!

Stop the EBOLA patients from
entering the U.S. Treat them,
at the highest level, over there.
THE UNITED STATES HAS
ENOUGH PROBLEMS!

*Whereas Africa just can't get enough problems. The grip of U.S.
Customs and Border Protection tightens ever further as Ebola patients
join Muslims as persona non grata in Don's brave new world.*

While @BetteMidler is an
extremely unattractive woman,
I refuse to say that because I always
insist on being politically correct.

*Never mind political correctness, Don insists on being correct at all
times, especially where matters of the opposite sex are concerned.*

All of the women on
The Apprentice flirted with me
– consciously or unconsciously.
That's to be expected.

They are only human, after all, and The Donald is a master at picking up on the telltale signs of unconscious flirting.

The U.S. has become a dumping ground for everybody else's problems. When Mexico sends its people, they're not sending their best. They're not sending you. They're sending people that have lots of problems, and they're bringing those problems to us. They're bringing drugs. They're bringing crime. They're rapists. And some, I assume, are good people.

Drugs and rape fail to make any official list of Mexico's chief exports, which can only point to a conspiracy. Perhaps these assumed 'good people' can be the insiders to help Don finally expose his truth.

I will build a great wall — and nobody builds walls better than me, believe me — and I'll build them very inexpensively. I will build a great, great wall on our southern border, and I will make Mexico pay for that wall. Mark my words.

Trump extends the olive branch by building an inexpensive wall for Mexico to pay for so they can keep their drugs and rapists in check.

Rosie O'Donnell's disgusting both inside and out. You take a look at her, she's a slob. She talks like a truck driver, she doesn't have her facts, she'll say anything that comes to her mind.

Oh, Don. Maybe if you really got to know her…

If I were running *The View*, I'd fire
Rosie O'Donnell. I mean, I'd look
at her right in that fat, ugly face
of hers, I'd say 'Rosie, you're fired'.

The gentleman doth protest too much. Does he have a soft spot for Rosie?

Cher is somewhat of a loser. She's lonely, she's unhappy, she's very miserable, and her sound-enhanced and computer-enhanced music doesn't do it for me, believe me.

Well, if she wasn't lonely, unhappy and miserable before, she surely will be when she learns Donald doesn't like her music.

Sadly, because President Obama has done such a poor job as president, you won't see another black president for generations!

It could be worse, Don — it might be a woman next.

I think the only difference between
me and the other candidates is
that I'm more honest and my
women are more beautiful.

*To be fair, they might be able to count the two differences you
describe, Don. And maybe they don't consider 'their' women to
be possessions. But yeah, sure, otherwise you're the same.*

Isn't it interesting that the tragedy in Paris took place in one of the toughest gun control countries in the world?

No tragedy is too great for Donald to defend his views on guns. The answer is clearly more guns — many more of them. How could we have been so stupid?

My fingers are long and beautiful, as, it has been well documented, are various other parts of my body.

*In response to **Spy** magazine's labelling him a 'short-fingered vulgarian', Don delivered this elegant and not-at-all stomach-churning riposte. Yes, Don, but what about the girth?*

My Twitter has become so
powerful that I can actually
make my enemies tell the truth.

The force is strong with this one. Trump's social-media mind games are surely too
powerful for the average bleeding heart liberal or Rosie O'Donnell to take.

The point is that you can't be too greedy.

*The film **Wall Street**, featuring Gordon Gekko and his immortal line 'Greed is good', was released in 1987, the same year that Don's opus **The Art of the Deal**, featuring this similar riff, hit the shelves. **Wall Street** didn't finish with Gekko running to be a candidate for president, however, proving that the truth always Trumps fiction.*

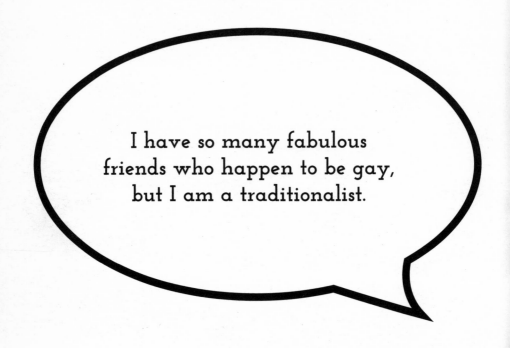

I have so many fabulous
friends who happen to be gay,
but I am a traditionalist.

Gay marriage, a thorny issue for some, but hardly for Donald. He rolls out a
classic 'I have lots of [insert your own minority here] friends, but…' line to prove
he's not narrow minded — he even calls them fabulous! — but he is traditional.

The other candidates — they went in, they didn't know the air conditioning didn't work. They sweated like dogs... How are they gonna beat ISIS? I don't think it's gonna happen.

Air conditioning engineers all over America are being recruited as part of Trump's foreign policy.

66 China's Communist Party has now publicly praised Obama's reelection. They have never had it so good. Will own America soon. 99

Don indulges in some Cold War nostalgia as 'the Reds' are coming once again

66 He's not a war hero. He's a war hero because he was captured. I like people that weren't captured, OK? I hate to tell you. 99

Don tells it how it is on John McCain's war record. Or at least how it is from his draft-deferring perch on sofa watching Platoon and Apocalypse Now, the only Vietnam action Trump saw.

I've read hundreds of books about China over the decades. I know the Chinese. I've made a lot of money with the Chinese. I understand the Chinese mind.

Know thine enemy, or at least arrogantly assume thou does, is how Don likes to pimp legendary Chinese warrior Sun Tzu's prose.

He may have one, but there is something on that birth certificate. Maybe religion. Maybe it says he's a Muslim. I don't know. Maybe he doesn't want that. Or he may not have one. I will tell you this: if he wasn't born in this country, it's one of the great scams of all time.

The hours spent in conspiracy chat rooms on the internet finally pay off as Trump manages to sound like a man wearing a sandwich board ranting on a street corner about the apocalypse or religion or the greatest trick the devil ever pulled.

Sorry losers and haters, but, my IQ is one of the highest — and you all know it! Please don't feel so stupid or insecure; it's not your fault.

Don't hate the player, hate the game, losers and haters — especially if the game is bragging about your IQ without actually stating a number.

We build a school, we build a road, they blow up the school, we build another school, we build another road, they blow them up, we build again, in the meantime we can't get a fucking school in Brooklyn.

Fittingly for a speech about Iraq, The Donald drops the F-bomb for maximum devastation.

We have nobody in Washington that sits back and says, 'You're not going to raise that fucking price.'

Don's F-bomb lands on OPEC this time.

I saw a report yesterday. There's so much oil, all over the world, they don't know where to dump it. And Saudi Arabia says, 'Oh, there's too much oil.' Do you think they're our friends? They're not our friends.

Don doesn't want to play with Saudi Arabia so there.

Does anyone care what this man [Alex Salmond] thinks? He's a has-been and totally irrelevant.

The fact that he doesn't even know what's going on in his own constituency says it all. We have a permanent clubhouse and the business is flourishing.

He should go back to doing what he does best – unveiling pompous portraits of himself that pander to his already overinflated ego.

Break-ups can be so painful, but surely Alex Salmond knew this day was coming.

Sources

p. 6: https://www.youtube.com/watch?v=diMp24lgAcw

p. 8: an interview with Esquire, 1991 http://www.huffingtonpost.com/entry/18-real-things-donald-trump-has-said-about-women_us_55d356a8e4b07addcb442023

p. 11: Twitter

p. 13: http://www.huffingtonpost.com/2011/03/21/donald-trump-gaddafi-screwed_n_838328.html

p. 14: Twitter

p. 16: http://www.huffingtonpost.com/2013/05/08/donald-trump-tweet-sexual-assault-military_n_3239781.html

p. 18: Twitter

p. 19: Twitter

p. 20: http://www.theatlantic.com/politics/archive/2011/04/donald-trump-i-have-a-great-relationship-with-the-blacks/237332/

p. 22: http://abcnews.go.com/Politics/donald-trump-president-trump-weighs-sheen-palin-obama/story?id=13154163

p. 25: http://www.cityam.com/218071/donald-trump-run-us-president-2016-claims-i-beat-china-all-time

p. 26: Twitter

p. 29: Twitter

p. 30: http://edition.cnn.com/2016/01/07/politics/donald-trump-guns-obama-town-hall/

p. 33: Twitter
http://www.theguardian.com/tv-and-radio/tvandradioblog/2012/dec/07/donald-trump-alan-sugar-twitter-fight

p. 34: Twitter

p. 36: http://www.etonline.com/news/167197_exclusive_donald_trump_addresses_anti_immigration_comments_i_don_t_have_a_racist_bone_my_body/

p. 39: Twitter

p. 40: Twitter

p. 42: http://edition.cnn.com/2015/12/07/politics/donald-trump-muslim-ban-immigration/

p. 44: http://www.huffingtonpost.com/steve-young/we-must-take-trump-seriou_b_7661164.html

p. 46: https://www.youtube.com/watch?v=wN7KHWdyrbI

p. 48 (top): Twitter

p. 48 (bottom): http://www.huffingtonpost.com/entry/donald-trump-plutocrat-populist_us_55afcf39e4b0a9b948534f21

p. 50: https://www.donaldjtrump.com/press-releases/donald-j.-trump-response-to-the-pope

p. 52: https://www.donaldjtrump.com/press-releases/donald-j.-trump-response-to-the-pope

p. 55 (top): Twitter

p. 55 (bottom): Twitter

p. 56: https://www.washingtonpost.com/news/book-party/wp/2015/08/05/donald-trump-on-women-sex-marriage-and-feminism/

p. 58: https://www.youtube.com/watch?v=q_q6lB-DyPk

p. 60: http://www.msnbc.com/msnbc/donald-trump-says-his-wall-would-cost-8-billion

p. 62: http://gothamist.com/2006/12/21/rosie_odonnell_1.php

p. 64: Entertainment Tonight Interview https://www.washingtonpost.com/news/the-fix/wp/2015/07/22/quiz-did-donald-trump-say-this-outrageous-quote-or-no/

p. 67: http://www.mediaite.com/tv/trump-responds-to-chers-attack-on-romney-shes-somewhat-of-a-loser-whos-very-miserable/

p. 68: Twitter

p. 69: http://www.nytimes.com/1999/11/17/opinion/liberties-living-la-vida-trumpa.html

p. 71: https://www.washingtonpost.com/news/post-politics/wp/2015/11/14/donald-trump-says-tough-gun-control-laws-in-paris-contributed-to-tragedy/

p. 72: http://nypost.com/2011/04/03/trump-card/

http://www.people.com/article/donald-trump-fingers-small-vanity-fair-hands

p. 74: Twitter

p. 77: http://uk.businessinsider.com/donald-trump-business-philosophy-from-the-art-of-the-deal-2015-6?r=US&IR=T

p. 78: http://bit.ly/1OxLOW9

p. 80: http://www.politico.com/story/2015/06/donald-trump-2016-announcement-10-best-lines-119066

p. 83 (top): Twitter

p. 83 (bottom): http://www.thedailybeast.com/articles/2015/07/18/draft-dodging-trump-says-pow-mccain-not-a-war-hero.html

p. 84: http://latimesblogs.latimes.com/washington/2011/05/donald-trump-i-understand-the-chinese-mind.html

p. 87: http://www.huffingtonpost.com/2011/03/31/donald-trump-obama-birth-_n_843056.html

p. 88 (top): Twitter

P. 88 (bottom): http://www.nationalreview.com/article/266253/donald-trumps-f-bombs-dennis-prager

p. 90: http://www.nationalreview.com/article/266253/donald-trumps-f-bombs-dennis-prager

http://www.liberalamerica.org/2015/09/03/watch-donald-trump-saying-listen-you-mother-fckers-to-the-chinese-people/

p.93: http://bit.ly/1W0cAyf

p. 94: http://www.bbc.co.uk/news/uk-scotland-scotland-politics-35113085